HOW YOUR PROPERTY TAX

Practical tips from a property tax professional

By Daniel Thomas Jones

Managing Director
Fair Assessments, LLC
Atlanta, GA 30341
FairAssessments.com

Copyright 2013 Daniel Thomas Jones

Limit of Liability/Disclaimer of Warranty

While the author has used best efforts in preparing this book, the author makes no representations or warranties with respect to the accuracy or completeness of the contents of this book and specifically disclaims any implied warranties of merchantability or fitness for a particular purpose. The advice and strategies contained herein may not be suitable for every situation. This work is sold with the understanding that the author is not engaged in rendering professional services such as legal, accounting, or other. You should consult with a professional where appropriate. The fact that an organization or website is referred to in this work as a citation and/or a potential source of further information does not mean that the author endorses the information that the organization or website may provide or recommendations it may make. The author shall not be liable for any loss of profit or any other commercial damages, including but not limited to special, incidental, consequential, or other damages. No warranty may be created or extended by sales or promotional materials.

Table of contents

Preface

Part 1 The skinny

Part 2 Here's the beef

Part 3 Grade A help

Part 4 Conclusion

Preface

Congratulations on your decision to invest in my book, *"How to Appeal Your Property Tax."*
For the last nine years, my full time job has been helping people appeal their property tax assessments. During that time I worked property tax appeals in 19 states, primarily on the East Coast from Florida to Maine. While the vast majority of these appeals have been in commercial property values, I have extensive experience in helping people like you appeal their residential values. I have also worked on the other side of the appeals process. For eight years I was on the staffs of two county assessment departments in Prince William County, Virginia and Fulton County, Georgia and generated the values those counties used to tax real estate owners. Because I've helped set assessments *and* file appeals, I am not exaggerating when I say I know the tax appeals process inside and out.

In 2010, I opened my own real estate valuation and analysis business, Fair Assessments LLC, in Atlanta. We specialize in helping property owners and tenants in the retail, office, apartment, single family, hospitality and industrial sectors reduce their property taxes. In working with these various groups, it became readily obvious to me that there are substantially more residential owners who need help than commercial owners. Another thing I learned is that I can't reach every residential property owner I would like to help from my office. That's when I decided to write this book. I thought it would be the best way to help as many homeowners as possible across the country reduce their property taxes. That's not to say this book doesn't apply to commercial property owners. It does, and wherever I have written "homeowner" there is a good chance it applies to commercial property, too. But, I get so many questions about residential tax assessments I decided that homeowners are the ones who need the most help in navigating the property tax appeals process.

One of the questions homeowners ask me again and again is when they should file an appeal. I always tell them they should appeal their property tax assessment when they don't know the rate at which they will be taxed. I also tell them it helps to understand how the taxing authority (city, county, etc.) determines that rate. Here's how it works on the government end. The taxing authority has a budget -- think of the budget as a revenue requirement -- to finance its operations. Tax assessors arrive at a property tax rate by dividing the revenue requirement by the total taxable value of the county or city in which you live. However, the assessors typically don't calculate this required rate until they have finished adjusting all of the values and until they know how much of the value is in dispute. As a result, they often will not publish the rate until after the deadline to appeal your taxable value has passed!

I also tell homeowners that tax rates may rise because real estate values have fallen. In cases of declining real estate values, the taxing authority increases the tax rate to generate the same amount of revenue that came in prior to the fall in real estate prices. This would be fine if all the values in the county or city were adjusted downward by the same percentage. Unfortunately, this is unlikely to happen. It's possible tax assessors may adjust values downward in many different market areas but not where you live. As a result, the total tax base will have declined, which will result in an increased tax rate. If your real estate value remains unchanged, the higher tax rate will result in a higher tax bill.

The examples above are a simplification because the taxing authority may use other revenue sources, such as sales taxes and the like, to determine rates. Property taxes, though, are generally the major source of revenue for city and county governments. If the tax assessors have been lowering values but they haven't lowered your value, then you should be proactive and appeal your assessment. Don't wait until the new tax rate is published to file an appeal only to find out that the appeal deadline has passed.

This book is divided into three sections.

Part 1: The Skinny. The opening section covers the basics of analyzing your taxable value. In these pages you will learn what data to provide the tax assessor and gain enough information to get you started and, perhaps, through the property tax appeals process.

Part 2: Here's the Beef. This section goes into much more detail than Part 1 about the real estate appraisal process and the mass appraisal process tax assessors use. This section also provides information about steps you need to take to support your request for a reduction in assessed value and what to expect at a formal property tax appeal hearing.

Part 3: Grade A Help. The concluding section offers information about property tax consultants. These are the people who will appeal your tax assessment for a fee.

Finally, at the end of the book you will find property tax resources for all 50 states and the District of Columbia. I've included a link to a website for each state. The link will take you to a page that provides information on the property tax process and/or appeal procedures for that state.

You've no doubt heard the saying that "nothing is certain in life but death and taxes." This book doesn't include anything about death, but I think you'll find the information about taxes useful! You can find additional information at Fair-Assessments.com. Now let's start reading and save some money.

Part one: The skinny

Chapter 1
Researching tax assessments

The first order of business in trying to decide whether to appeal your property tax assessment is to get a copy of your tax assessment property record card and check it for accuracy.

In doing this, be aware that the tax assessment personnel probably haven't looked at your property in years. In fact, there's a good chance they haven't looked at it since it was a new structure. Many counties have tens or even hundreds of thousands of parcels of land. Most assessors are so busy "picking up" new construction that they don't have the staff or the time to look at every property on a regular basis.

Step one: Check the assessed value
Because the city or county probably hasn't reviewed your property in years, you should carefully check the tax assessor's description before you appeal their assessed value. What you are looking for in the property description is misinformation that inflates the assessed value of your property. That could be the basis to file an appeal. On the other hand, if the assessor's description doesn't include the screen porch, finished basement or other improvements you've made, you should think twice about inviting a county appraiser to look at your property.

Assessed value is the taxable value. Assessed value sometimes differs from market value, or what your real estate is actually worth, due to fractional assessment laws. Some states assess property at 100 percent of market value. Others play with the numbers. Georgia, for example, has a 40 percent assessment. This means that a property valued at $100,000 will be taxed on an assessment of $40,000. Why would states use this type of formula? It's beyond me. Fractional assessments just result in higher tax rates to make up the difference in revenue that an assessment at 100 percent of market value would produce.

States that use fractional assessments often list both the market value estimate and the fractional assessment on their tax assessment notices. If your taxing authority only provides the fractional assessment, you can compute the market value by dividing the assessment by the fractional assessment ratio. For example if our Georgia assessment notice shows an assessment of $40,000 and we know that Georgia assesses at 40 percent of market value, then to obtain the market value estimate we divide $40,000 by 0.40 which gives us the $100,000 market value. The important thing to remember is that if your state uses fractional assessments, you should compare apples to apples. Compare assessed values to assessed values and market values to market values. Not one to the other.

Step two: Determine comparables

To determine if your tax assessment is correct, research properties in your neighborhood that are similar to yours. You will be looking for two things that tax assessors call "comparables:"
1. The sale price of properties similar to yours.
2. The assessed value (equity) of similar properties.

Compare the information you find in the comparables to the taxable value on your property. This will let you know whether the assessed value of your property is reasonable and fair.

To find sale prices of properties similar to yours, look at the tax assessor's website for your county or city. Many tax assessors have excellent websites, and you should be able to see your property description, the descriptions for your neighbor's property as well as sales information for your neighborhood or your market area. If the tax assessor's website doesn't show sales data, contact their office and ask if they have sales data you can come in and look through.

There are other options to finding sale prices. You can ask a realtor friend to pull some comparable sales. If you have a neighborhood association and you're not familiar with the sales in the neighborhood, you might bring up the subject of property tax appeals at your next meeting. Ask your neighbors if they're aware of any sales that might support lower taxable values. You might also search the Internet for sales information at websites of established realtor organizations such as the National Association of Realtors. Before using sales you find in online real estate databases, compare them to the tax assessor's data to verify the sale price and sale date information.

Equity is something you can only research at the tax assessor's website or office because equity is all about fairness. It answers the question: Is your tax assessment reasonable compared to similar properties in your market area? Therefore, the tax assessors will have that data. Equity is not an approach to value, yet for assessment purposes it can be as important as one.

Most states that I have worked in require taxing jurisdictions to assess property value based on equity, or "uniformity." They do this is to ensure that the tax burden is distributed fairly. The states that are exceptions that I know of that do not consider equity a valid argument when appealing taxable value are Florida and Ohio. I have worked property tax appeals in many states on the east coast, but not all. Other states may not consider equity a valid reason to file an appeal. Always ask your local tax assessor.

When considering equity start with the assessor's property records. Look through the assessed values of properties in your neighborhood. Find a handful or as many as 10-20 properties that have lower assessments than your property. Dig in, either online or at the assessor's office. Look for reasons these properties are valued lower than yours. Are they smaller, with fewer amenities? Has your property been given a higher quality rating for no apparent reason? Is your property newer? Or, has your property been given a higher condition rating than the competition for no apparent reason? These are just a few examples of assessor data points that could be inequitable.

That's equity in a nutshell. Be aware that developing an equity argument not only can be time-consuming, but in many states the equity argument alone does not get positive results for homeowners. You must have some sales, a cost approach or an income approach (more on this in Part 2) that support a lower value. Then you can present an equity argument in support of the lower value.

Step three: Establish units of comparison

After you have comparables for sale comparison and equity, some of which hopefully will support a lower value than what the tax assessor has determined for your property, you will need to express those sale prices and assessments in appropriate units of comparison. The most appropriate single family residential unit of comparison is sale price or assessment per square foot of living area (SFLA). SFLA is finished, heated living area that is above grade. Above grade means that the lowest level of the floor is above ground. Some assessors may include a finished, heated basement in the SFLA. You will have to ask your assessor's office about their policy if it is unclear to you whether a finished basement is included in the SFLA. There isn't anything wrong with this approach, as long as all properties are being treated the same.

Expressing assessments and sale prices in terms of units of comparison often eliminates the need to make any adjustment for size. Assessors and appraisers measure buildings from the outside, using the exterior walls. If you want to check the accuracy of the assessor's estimate of your SFLA, measure your building the same way. For those sale comparables that were not obtained from the assessor, you will have to look up the assessor's square footage, unless, for example, you want to measure your neighbor's houses or your competitor's retail stores.

Step four: Determine medians and averages

When you have your sale and equity comparables in the appropriate unit of comparison, then you will need to look at some statistics associated with those. For example, look at the median sale price per square foot of living area for houses. Assessors always look at medians, rather than averages, because medians are unaffected by extreme values, which are also called outliers. Median, as you remember, is the midpoint of a group of numbers arranged in ascending or descending order. When there is an even number of values, the two middle values are averaged to obtain the median. You want to compare these numbers, the median sale price per SFLA and median assessment per SFLA to the assessment per square foot of living area on your property. This will give you an idea of whether your property is assessed fairly or if the assessment is too high or too low. For example, consider the comparables in the chart below:

Address	Sale Date	Sale Price	SFLA	Price/SF	Year Built
123 Main Street	Oct-10	$375,000	3,272	$114.61	1985
456 Pine Street	Mar-10	$450,000	2,722	$165.32	1989
789 Oak Street	Mar-10	$525,000	3,536	$148.47	1995
234 Cedar Lane	Feb-10	$555,000	3,373	$164.54	2000
12618 Maple Court	Mar-10	$900,000	5,946	$151.36	1991
345 Applewood Road	Jun-10	$1,060,000	7,000	$151.43	1995
			Median	$151.40	
			Average	$149.29	
1054 River Birch Road	Assessment	$644,400	3,458	$186.35	1990

In this case, the average and median sale prices per foot are very similar as there is no outlier sale included in our sample of six comparable sales. Here it is readily apparent that the subject property, River Birch Road, is over valued at $186.35 per foot. A more reasonable value is indicated by the average and median sale prices of approximately $150 per foot. This yields a recommended value of $518,700 and a tax assessment reduction of $125,700, or 19.5 percent.

Below is a similar analysis using assessments, or equity:

Address	Assessment	SFLA	Total $/SF	Year built
1050 River Birch Road	$505,000	3,327	$151.79	1990
1052 River Birch Road	$555,000	3,720	$149.19	1990
1062 River Birch Road	$610,000	4,210	$144.89	1991
12760 Maple Court	$655,000	4,563	$143.55	1999
		Median	$147.04	
		Average	$147.36	
1054 River Birch Road	$644,400	3,458	$186.35	1990

Here there are four comparable properties with lower tax assessments per foot of living area than the subject property. As we are working with tax assessments in the same market area, there should be no extreme values. As in the previous example, the average and median assessments per foot are very similar. Based on these equity comparables, the subject property, 1054 River Birch Road, should be valued at approximately $147 per foot. This yields a recommended value of $508,326 and a tax reduction of $136,074, or 21 percent.

If you cannot find really good comparables for your property, "bracket" your property with superior and inferior comparables. Use comparables that are larger and smaller, in better and worse condition, or older and newer. This will make the median price per foot, or assessment per foot, reasonable in relation to your property.

Chapter 2
When to appeal

When and how to appeal property tax assessments varies by state. Most states have specific dates when appeals can be filed. Some states, on the other hand, permit property tax appeals at any time. Some states let you appeal by a simple letter as long as you include information in the appeal, such as the property tax assessor's parcel identification number, that identifies the property in a way the taxing authority will accept. Other states require you to fill out a specific form to file an appeal.

For links to property tax information in each of the 50 states and the District of Columbia, please see the appendix. Remember, though, that regulations can change, so you should always contact your local assessor's office to get the most up-to-date information.

Here are some examples of how the appeals process works in several Southern states.

Alabama
Assessments can be appealed by letter to the county Board of Equalization. When the Board of Equalization finishes reviewing and adjusting values, the assessor publishes the result and the homeowner has 10 days to appeal. However, homeowners should always check with their local taxing authority to find out how much time they have to file an appeal and when they should appeal.

Florida
Assessments can be appealed by letter, although a state appeal form is also available. The counties mail taxable values in TRIM (truth in millage) notices in August and September. Homeowners have 30 days to appeal to the Value Adjustment Board, although personnel from the county assessor's office (called the county Property Appraiser statewide) will review the appeal informally before any formal hearing. Florida's Value Adjustment Boards have a filing fee. The fee is typically $15. TRIM notices are sent on every property annually.

Georgia

Values hit the mail in April and continue coming out through June. Homeowners have 45 days to appeal from the date on the notice. Appeals can be made by letter or on a state appeal form. Assessment notices are sent on every property annually.

North Carolina

The tax assessment notices are mailed infrequently and dates vary by county. After they come out, homeowners have 30 days from the date on the notice to file an appeal. There is typically a county appeal form that must be used. North Carolina is on an eight-year reappraisal cycle, which means that counties must reappraise at least once every eight years. Consequently, there are long periods of time between reappraisals. Typically, if homeowners appeal in a non-reappraisal year they have to do it early in the year, prior to April 30. Homeowners should check with their county tax assessor for appeals dates and deadlines.

South Carolina

Tax assessment notices are mailed infrequently, and dates vary by county. After the notices come out, homeowners have 90 days to appeal. South Carolina is on a four-year reappraisal cycle, which means there are four years between each revaluation. If it's not a reappraisal year, homeowners can appeal at any time.

Don't guess about processes or deadlines. I can't stress this enough. Be an informed taxpayer! Call your county assessor's office and find out when the tax assessment notices are coming out and how much time there is to appeal. Call your state revenue or finance office or visit the website regarding state law on property tax to find out the frequency of reappraisals and what you can expect. To help you get started, there is a list by state of websites with property tax information in the appendix of this book.

Chapter 3
Preparing for a property tax appeal

Homeowners should always protect their rights during an appeals process. There are several ways to do this.

Always file a property tax appeal in writing. Don't go to the tax assessor's office and begin discussing a home's value with the personnel. That just gives the staff a chance to say "thanks for the information, we'll get back to you." By the time that happens, the property tax appeal deadline may have passed. At that point, if you're not satisfied with what they tell you, there is nothing else that you can do for that tax year. By following the simple steps in this chapter, homeowners will always have a second option, a way to further their appeal if they're not happy with the initial response from the tax assessors.

The information you gathered while researching the property tax assessment (Chapter 1) can be the basis to appeal your property tax assessment. Provided the sales information supported a lower value, or sales and equity comparables supported a lower value, this may be all that is needed to get a reduction in the property's taxable value. You won't know until you try. If the assessor's response is unsatisfactory, a presentation will be needed at the second level of appeal (more on this in Part 2).

The information that tax assessors require for an appeal varies by state and county. Sometimes they want all of the information for a tax appeal to be filed at the time of the appeal. In other cases, there may be no such requirement. Some states may not require any supporting information. In states or counties that require all of the supporting information to be filed at the time of the appeal, the county appraiser should also be required to disclose all of the information they'll be using. If this isn't the case, then the deck is being stacked against you. Check with your state revenue or finance department, or look for contact information at the website provided in the appendix of this book, if this is what you are being told.

I like to say "don't show your hand" when discussing how much information to give to the tax assessor. When filing an appeal or when approaching the appropriate assessment personnel to discuss an appeal, only supply them with the minimal information to prove that the tax assessment is high. If homeowners give the assessor's office everything they have, that gives the taxing authority an opportunity to build a case to deny the appeal that they can present later at a formal hearing. Save some information for a second level of appeal, typically a formal hearing, so that the county appraiser doesn't have all of the evidence ahead of time. If you are required to submit all information with your initial appeal this is not possible.

Remember, too, that county appraisers are busy right now due to the real estate depression. There have been large numbers of appeals filed during the past several years. Homeowners don't have to spend a lot of time preparing a complete presentation when providing just some information to the county appraiser may result in a satisfactory reduction. Something else to keep in mind that may work in your favor is that if the county has large numbers of appeals, then the county appraisers may be under pressure to settle as many appeals as possible prior to spending time on formal hearings.

Chapter 4
Contacting the tax assessor

After filing a property tax appeal, call the tax assessor's office, get the name of the appraiser responsible for your market area or neighborhood and ask for an appointment. Present the supporting information at this meeting rather than supplying it with the written appeal (if possible). There's a strategic reason for doing this: Don't give information to the appraiser and let them form an opinion before you have a chance to talk with them.

If the appraiser is hesitant to meet with you, drive by the tax assessor's office to drop off the information and ask if the appropriate appraiser is available. Maybe you'll get a few minutes to talk with them at that point.

Here's another possible scenario: The appraiser says he or she won't meet with you but is willing to negotiate over the phone. In that case, ask if you can email or fax your information to them, and then follow up with a phone call to discuss the information soon afterward.

Strategies to make your case
If possible I recommend that you give the county appraiser as little information that makes your case as possible. This is typically three comparables, whether sales or equity, or both. Appraisers like to say "one sale doesn't make a market," and that's why they typically use at least three comparables.

Settle before a formal hearing
In my experience, it is worthwhile to discuss the appeal with the appropriate appraiser rather than go before a board at a formal hearing. There is no way to predict what will happen at a formal hearing. The assessment personnel work with these boards day in and day out, and they have a friendly relationship. Imagine what will happen if you show up having never seen nor talked to the appraiser and the appraiser has good data supporting the assessed value. Even if you have good data supporting your value, you are a stranger to everyone. Whose side do you think the Board will take? In some

states the tax assessor is presumed correct by law, unless the property owner can prove otherwise.

Be open to compromise

Be willing to settle somewhere in the middle. The county may have sales that support a $200,000 value, and maybe you have some sales that support a $150,000 value. By settling in the middle you will save time for yourself and the county as well. You know you're using the lowest sales available. You know they're using the highest sales available. Remember median and average? Settle somewhere in the middle, unless it is obvious your property is below average in some way that affects value.

Be polite

Also, don't be combative or condescending towards the tax ' assessment personnel. That kind of attitude won't help your case if you have to meet them again at a formal hearing. Many people have an attitude towards government employees. I have worked for two different counties and I believe that the vast majority of appraisers know their jobs well.

Be persistent

Because of the recent real estate depression, counties and cities all over the country have had large numbers of property tax appeals. As a result, the county appraisers may be overwhelmed and behind. I know some counties have so many appeals that they are still working prior-year appeals even while their current year values have been released. Homeowners who want to file an appeal are going to have to be persistent. If the county appraiser has a huge stack of tax appeal folders and they can't even find yours, then you will have to call back every few weeks to ask about your value.

The next level of appeal

If you're not happy with what the tax assessors do for you, then there is a second level of appeal. This is often called a board of equalization, board of review, board of appeals, appellate tax board, etc. These boards are a second chance to get your property tax assessment, and tax bill, reduced. This is also an opportunity to try and work something out with the county appraiser again.

The second level of appeal is typically considered a formal hearing. Be forewarned. Formal hearings require some preparation on your part. However, if the county appraisers are busy, their heavy workload could work to your advantage. They may not be happy about having to take time away from a full schedule to prepare for a formal hearing. Thus, overflowing calendars may make them more amenable to settling with you.

Part two: Here's the beef

Chapter 5
A short history of property tax assessment

Property taxes have been around almost as long as civilization itself. The Egyptians, Greeks and far eastern civilizations levied property taxes primarily on land and its agricultural production. The more productive and profitable the land, the higher the tax. Historically, property taxes have been used to fund government expenditures.

Alexander the Great was not only a military genius, he also knew how to fund military excursions. Whenever the Greeks conquered a new land, they instituted a property tax system that would help fund additional military campaigns and other government expenditures. In this way, Alexander and the Greeks were able to control one of the largest land areas in the history of the world.

When the Pilgrims landed in America, they needed revenue to fund local government so they instituted what was familiar to them -- a property tax system. The settlers taxed real estate (land and buildings) and personal property such as horses and livestock. Proceeds were used to fund law enforcement, churches and schools.

Few people know that before he became the 16th president of the United States, Abraham Lincoln worked as an attorney and prosecuted several property tax appeal cases. He won several high profile cases for railroad and riverboat companies. I wonder if his tax reduction success helped him get elected to the highest office in the land.

Today, property taxes account for approximately 75 percent of local government revenue. Tax collections are used to pay for schools, road construction and maintenance, police and fire protection, the court system, public parks and many other government services. There is a saying that the only certain things in life are death and taxes, but at least we can minimize the impact that one of the two has on our lives!

Chapter 6
The Cost Approach

The tax assessor's job is to estimate *market value,* or some percentage of market value. Market value is defined as the most probable price a property would sell for, assuming that the buyer and seller are both knowledgeable, not under any undue pressure, and that the property is exposed to the open, competitive market for a typical marketing time.

Real estate appraisers and tax assessors use three recognized approaches to determine market value:

- The Cost Approach.
- The Sales Comparison Approach.
- The Income Approach.

The Cost Approach

Appraisers and assessor use three basic steps to implement the Cost Approach:

Step one: they estimate the cost to replace the improvements to the property using current construction standards and in current dollars. This is called a *cost-new estimate.*

Step two: From the cost-new estimate, they deduct an estimate of the total accrued depreciation on the subject property. This is called *depreciated cost new.*

Step three: To the depreciated cost new, they add an estimate of the value of the land. The number they arrive at in this final step is an estimate of the fair market value of the property.

Cost Approach... is based on the principle of substitution – that you would pay no more for a property than the cost to acquire a similar site and construct a building of equivalent utility in a reasonable time.

Most taxing jurisdictions use the Cost Approach to estimate market value of residential and commercial properties because it is relatively easy to automate.

Let's look at each of the steps in the Cost Approach in more detail:

Step one: The cost new estimate

In the Cost Approach, we estimate the *replacement cost new,* or the cost to build a structure of equivalent utility, using today's construction standards and current costs. This is in contrast to the sometimes-used *reproduction cost new,* which is the cost to build an exact replica, using the same construction standards of the original dwelling, no matter how outdated or inefficient they may be. In older homes it is impractical to use reproduction cost (think plaster walls and floor furnaces), so the tax assessors use replacement costs.

Step two: Depreciated cost new

After determining the replacement cost, the next step is to deduct a dollar amount for the total accrued depreciation on the property. Depreciation is a loss of value from any source. Depreciation is typically separated into three types:

1. Physical deterioration: due to age and use, or misuse and lack of maintenance.
2. Functional obsolescence is a loss in value due to over or under improvement, or outdated style. For example, houses with only two bedrooms have a functional problem in most market areas.
3. External obsolescence is a loss in value from outside of the property boundary. Proximity to a busy road or landfill are examples of external obsolescence, as is the closing of the largest employer in a town.

Deducting total accrued depreciation from the replacement cost estimate results in a *depreciated replacement cost new.*

Step three: Fair market value

The final step is to add an estimate of the site (land) value to the *depreciated replacement cost new* estimate. The number arrived at in this step provides an estimate of the fair market value of the property. Land is normally valued using the Sales Comparison Approach to value, which we will cover shortly.

The tax assessors use a *computer-assisted mass appraisal system (CAMA)* to aid in their appraisal of thousands of properties. The CAMA usually has a Cost Approach to value built into the software, which has a database with cost tables. Initially, the replacement costs in this database are based on recent cost data from a reliable published source. Property descriptions are put into the system and are assigned to different cost tables based on construction quality, condition, style, size, etc. In a relatively homogeneous neighborhood of one story, single family houses built by the same builder in a relatively short time-frame, all of the properties should be assigned to the same cost and depreciation tables.

County appraisers frequently insert some subjective elements into the cost approach. When neighborhoods are new, typically the properties in them are put in the system with the same quality codes. Over time, however, due to appeals or description updates, these quality ratings begin to change per property. Thus, you may find that your neighbor, who appealed his or her value last year, has a quality code of "B" while your house, built by the same builder in the same year, has a quality code of "A".

Usually all properties within a neighborhood are assigned to the same depreciation schedule, resulting in building values depreciating at the same rate. However, the county will usually assign a condition code to each property, which will alter this depreciation schedule. If you think that your property is in inferior condition compared with your neighbor's property with the same condition rating, this may be a good point to argue when appealing your tax assessment. Alternatively, if your neighbor/competitors property has a lower condition rating for no apparent reason, you can argue that your property's condition rating is unfair and should be lowered.

Appraisers use the cost approach all the time. Unless you are familiar with it, though, you're probably not going to be able to do it yourself. My suggestion is to obtain a copy of your property record card from the tax assessor's office. This will often have the cost approach to your property printed on it. You should be able to see the cost per foot they are using, what percentage depreciation is on it, and similar important factors. You can also take the comparable sales and equity comparables that you've identified and get the property record cards for those properties. Then you can compare the cost approach to see if your property is being valued at a higher cost per foot than the comparables, or if you're not being given as much depreciation as the comparables even though your house is the same age and building quality as the comparables.

Chapter 7
The Sales Comparison Approach

Sales Comparison Approach...estimates a property's
market value by comparing the property to similar,
recently sold properties. The sold properties are adjusted
to give an indication of what they would have sold for if
they were like the subject property.

This approach, like the name implies, compares a property to the sale of comparable properties in the market area. Keep in mind that adjustments must be made for differences in properties, such as the number of bathrooms, by adding (or subtracting) the approximate value of those differences to the sale price to get an indication of what the property might sell for. For example, if there is a sale that is just like the subject property except that it has one more bathroom, the property sold for $100,000 and the market values a bathroom at $4,000, then the indicated value of the subject property is $96,000.

Differences in properties are called *elements of comparison*, which is defined as characteristics that influence a buying decision and the price to be paid. In addition to the number of bathrooms, other elements of comparison that property owners should take into consideration are square footage, presence of basement, parking, etc. Once all of the comparable sales have been adjusted to get an indication of what they would have sold for if they were just like the subject property, then the data must reconciled in order to determine a value estimate on the subject property.

Typically, the sale that requires the least overall adjustment is given the most weight. This adjustment process is how a licensed, or fee appraiser would develop a value estimate by the Sales Comparison Approach. The tax assessors use comparable sales in a different way, which we will analyze in the chapter on Mass Appraisal.

Know your sales data
Be aware that when appealing taxable value, the county appraiser may bring sales data to an appeal hearing to support his or her CAMA-generated Cost Approach value. In these cases, they will

typically bring data from the most similar properties with the highest sale prices they can find. However, most tax assessment personnel are not licensed appraisers and do not have extensive experience creating Sales Comparison Approach analysis grids.

Even so, if property owners are going to engage in the appeals process they should be at least somewhat familiar with the Sales Comparison Approach. Unfortunately, unless the property owner is a real estate professional with access to real estate data services, they will have to do some digging to get the required data. One place to look for the sales data is on the assessor's website. Look for sales street-by-street in your neighborhood. This is the place to look for low-priced sales (bank sales, short sales) that may not appear on other, free websites. In some states, tax assessors will consider these types of sales in their analysis. In others, they are not considered indicators of *market value*. If the only sales in your neighborhood are bank sales, this may be the market and, as such, indicative of market value. There are a few free websites such as Trulia.com and Realtor.com that list sold properties. Always verify sale dates and prices with a second reliable source, such as the tax assessor records.

Search for the most recent sales that took place prior to the assessor's *effective date of appraisal*. This is January 1 in many states, but check the state information in the appendix at the end of this book for the date in your state and ask your local assessor to determine the effective date of appraisal in your county. Market values fluctuate over time, so an estimate of market value must be as of a date certain. Try to use sales that took place within the 12 months preceding the effective date of appraisal. For commercial properties, 24 months is not unreasonable. Identifying the lowest sales in your neighborhood is extremely important because the county will be using the highest sales they can find to support their values.

For the Sales Comparison Approach to value, it is important to use sales that are as similar to the subject property as possible. Then, those sales should be broken down into appropriate units of comparison, such as price per square foot of living area. As I said before, breaking the sales into units of comparison often eliminates any need to adjust for differences in size.

Once you have these numbers, the next step is to look at the median sales price per square foot of living area for a house. Always use median rather than average because average is affected by outliers or extreme values whereas the median is not. The median is what the assessors use, so property owners filing an appeal should also use it. Comparing the median sale price per foot to your assessment per foot will help determine whether your property is overvalued, undervalued or just right. This will also provide information to use in filing a property tax appeal if the assessed property value seems high.

Chapter 8
The Income Approach

Income Approach...is based on the principle of anticipation. The potential income that a property can produce is a major determinate of its value.

The Income Approach to value is used primarily on commercial properties. Assessors rarely use it on residential properties. When it is used on a residential property it usually is in a neighborhood with a very active rental market.

The Income Approach is basically a three-step process:

1. Step one is to estimate the potential income that the property can generate.
2. Step two is to estimate the net operating income (NOI). The way to do that is to estimate the operating expenses of the property and then deduct that amount from the estimated potential income.
3. Step three is to capitalize the net operating income into a value estimate. The capitalization rate is derived from sales of similar properties (comparables) and is an indication of how much investors are paying for a dollar of income from particular property types in particular market areas. Most CAMA systems have an Income Approach built in for the valuation of commercial properties.

The components of the Income Approach are:

Market rent: The dollar amount that a property would rent for if exposed to the open market.

Potential gross income: The annual income that a property would generate if fully occupied at a market rent.

Effective gross income: This is potential gross income less market vacancy (for the location and property type), collection losses, with the addition of any miscellaneous income the property can generate.

Operating expenses: The expenses required to continue the income-generating potential of the real estate.

Net operating income: The income remaining after operating expenses are deducted from effective gross income.

Capitalization rate: The rate used to capitalize net operating income into a value estimate. The capitalization rate is based on what market participants are paying for a particular property type in a specific market area.

Chapter 9
Equity

As previously discussed, equity is all about having a tax assessment that is fair when compared to the assessed value of properties of competitors or neighbors. Often, after many years of appraisals by different county appraisers, reappraisals and appeals in a neighborhood or market area, equity in assessments is forgotten or overlooked. Although it is a time-consuming argument to develop, often requiring the purchase of many assessor property record cards, the results can be worth the effort. It pays to make certain that your property tax burden is equitable, because frequently it is not.

I touched on the equity argument while discussing the three approaches to value. When I talked about having the same quality codes in the CAMA Cost Approach, or the same depreciation schedule, that's equity. Equity applies to commercial properties, too. When all neighborhood shopping centers in the same market area have the same market rent estimates, the same expense ratios and the same capitalization rate, that's equity.

Again, although equity is a good argument to make in most states, the best arguments often include another approach to value.

Chapter 10
Researching commercial tax assessments

Information in Chapter 1 regarding researching tax assessments using sale and equity comparables is generally true for commercial tax assessments. However, it will be harder to obtain sales data for commercial properties than for residential properties unless the tax assessors have good, accessible records. Commercial sales are available by subscription on the Internet at several sites, including LoopNet.com and CoStar.com.

Assessors should use fair market rents to estimate fair market value of commercial properties. Current asking and recently contracted rents may be different than they were several years ago. The taxing authority will want to see profit and loss information from commercial property owners. Be aware that if the rents are high, they may balk at the assessment reduction request. Property owners who have long term tenants whose rents were established near the top of the market will need to make a case that they aren't getting current market rents. They will need to prove that market rents are lower than what they are currently getting. Again, those who are not a real estate professional will have to do some digging. One place to do that digging is online at sites such as LoopNet and CoStar. When researching market rents, it is important to keep search parameters in the same market area and in the same property type.

Expect to pay a fee
It is hard to research operating expenses without paying a fee. RealtyRates.com sells a market survey that includes expense ratios for some property types in some market areas. Tax assessors typically use expense ratios from a published source. The county may have, for example, all warehouse properties appraised with a 15 percent operating expense ratio (15 percent of *effective gross income*). They may be unwilling to change this ratio for individual properties. But if you have a property with a special situation that results in consistently higher than typical operating expenses, then by all means bring it to their attention. Your actual operating income

and expense statements may have influence on the tax assessment personnel.

Some expenses that the IRS allows for calculating income tax are not allowed as operating expenses for appraisal or tax assessment purposes. For example:

1. Depreciation is an accounting expense. It's a gift from the government. It is not considered an operating expense and should not be deducted from your effective gross income.
2. Interest on debt is a financing expense. This is also called debt service.
3. Property taxes are normally included, but not for property tax purposes. This is because the assessors don't want last year's tax affecting the current year tax rate (more on this below).
4. Capital improvements, such as additions, are temporary charges and are not considered operating expenses.
5. Owner's expenses, such as personal income tax or the work your landscaper does at your home, are not considered operating expenses.

In the Income Approach, the deductions from gross income are typical and reasonable operating expenses, and taxes are considered typical and reasonable expense items. However, for tax assessment purposes, the taxes are not known. The values are being established so that the tax rate can be calculated for the current year. If the assessor is establishing a value for 2013 and is doing it at the beginning of the year, the tax rate is typically not known yet. If they are to include a tax component in the Income Approach as an operating expense, then they would have to use the prior year's tax amount. Because the Income Approach and resulting value is going to have an impact on the current year's tax rate, last year's tax would affect the new tax rate. As a result, there is a circular argument against using last year's tax in the Income Approach.

Instead of including property tax as an expense item, the tax assessors add their effective tax rate to the appropriate capitalization rate for a particular property type in a particular market area. This gives a property tax component influence on the final value, but it's not used as an operating expense and it's not used as an actual number, such as the prior year's tax amount. The loaded capitalization rate is then applied to all net income produced by the property, which, in turn, produces a value estimate.

Unless a property owner filing an appeal is willing to spend some money, capitalization rate information will not be easy to acquire. Ideally, these rates are derived from sold properties, where the *net operating income* and sale price are known. Appraisers and research firms spend a lot of time verifying the information on commercial sales and trying to ascertain the capitalization rate. Capitalization rate information is available from published sources such as RealtyRates, CoStar, LoopNet and others. One thing to keep in mind is that the higher the "cap rate" the lower the property value. Conversely, the lower the cap rate, the higher the property value.

Developing a value estimate

If you're an income property owner, you will want to use your own profit and loss information to develop a value estimate to see if it supports a lower tax assessment. Although the assessors want to use market data rather than data that is specific to a particular property, they will often consider data from an individual property. If, however, current market data supports a lower value than what the property's actual profit and loss indicates, then use market data.

If the tax assessor's property record card has an Income Approach on it, you can compare the rental rate being used to your actual rate, and the vacancy rate to your actual rate, etc. You also want to compare the Income Approach that the assessor has done on your property record card to your competition's property record cards to determine whether the rental rate that the assessor is using on your property is reasonable compared to your competition. You can check on whether your expense ratio and capitalization rate are reasonable as well.

You can also use units of comparison when analyzing commercial values. However, they will likely be much more variable than what is seen when analyzing residential values. This is because it is much more unusual to find commercial properties rather than residential properties that are similar in year built, size, quality of construction, height, build-out, etc. As a result, averages and medians for commercial properties may be far apart. Remember that tax assessors use the median, and you should too. The median is unaffected by crazy high or low values.

Units of comparison for commercial properties differ by property type. While every property can be looked at as price per foot of building area, some property types have more appropriate units of comparison. For example, there is sale price or assessment per guest room for hotels, and sale price or assessment per seat for restaurants. This makes sense if you think about it. The large square footage of a hotel is of no consequence if there are only 10 guest rooms. Because each seat or guest room has its own potential to generate income, buyers and sellers are more likely to analyze value using these units of comparison.

Just as in the first chapter on researching tax assessments, you should find sale and equity comparables (where possible) and analyze your property value in relation to the median sale price per unit of comparison and assessed value per unit of comparison for the comparables found. This is more difficult with commercial properties. But, with variability there is opportunity. Commercial values fall in a greater range than residential values. Generally speaking, commercial tax assessment personnel understand this. They often are more willing to grant reductions, within reason, than residential tax assessment personnel. This is because the residential appraisers generally have a lot more sales data and are more certain of their values.

Chapter 11
Mass appraisal

Although the tax assessors use the three approaches to value that have been discussed previously in this section, they use them in the context of *mass appraisal*. Mass appraisal is the appraisal of a universe of properties using computer models and testing those models using statistics. The tax assessors often start with a Cost Approach because it is very easy to automate. Once they have established Cost Approach values on all the properties, they compare Cost Approach values to the sale prices for those properties that have sold. This is called a *sale ratio study*, or the ratio of assessment to sale price.

In mass appraisal, when sales are used to generate market values they are typically used to adjust the Cost Approach values. For example, if all properties are valued using the Cost Approach, and on average the county's sold properties have Cost Approach values that are 80 percent of sale prices, they may raise their *cost tables* inside the CAMA system by 10 percent. The resulting *sale ratios* would show that assessments are now approximately 90 percent of sale prices. In effect, the Cost Approach is being changed by the sales, and there is no real Sales Comparison Approach used by the tax assessors in the mass appraisal process.

As previously stated, most CAMA systems have an Income Approach built in. The assessment personnel would collect market data on rental rates, expense ratios and capitalization rates. Using the property descriptions they have inside CAMA, values would be generated based on building type, size, condition, market area and the rates and ratios input into CAMA. Generally the Income Approach stands alone, but where sales data is plentiful, the sale prices of the sold properties can be compared to their Income Approach values to determine whether the Income Approach model is generating reasonable values.

The secret about mass appraisal
Here's a secret: Mass appraisal is unreliable. Heck, even an individual appraisal from a licensed appraiser is just one person's

estimate of fair market value. What do you think happens when you throw a few hundred properties into the mix, don't inspect any of them and use statistics to make decisions? You get a real loose estimate. County appraisers use the sold properties in a neighborhood or market area to create sale ratios. They use the median sale ratio from the market area to make decisions about the level of assessment (value). They use the coefficient of dispersion (COD), or average deviation about the median, to make decisions about confidence in their "sale ratio study." The International Association of Assessing Officers says that single-family CODs should be 15.0 or less and for homogenous areas should be 10.0 or less. Commercial property CODs should be 20.0 or less, and in large, urban counties should be 15.0 or less. COD information should be part of the public record. The public record is just that -- public. Use it! If the tax assessor's COD is high in your market area, then their median sale ratio that is impacting your assessment is unreliable.

Tax assessors are either political animals or they answer to political animals. The tax assessors are concerned with market value, but they are equally concerned about the tax digest as a whole. This can cause unofficial policies of "values can never be lower than last year" or "don't reduce anything more than 10 percent." Another problem that results from political pressure is called a price-related differential. This is what happens when there are higher levels of assessment in the wealthy parts of town and relatively low levels of assessment in the poorer parts of town. Conversely, a price-related differential occurs when lower-priced properties have the higher level of assessment and higher-priced properties have a lower level of assessment.

Chapter 12
Boards of equalization/review

If the assessors don't lower your value or don't lower it enough to satisfy your goals, then you have to take your appeal to the second level. Most states have multiple levels of appeal and there will be a deadline for the second level of appeal just like there was for the first. In this and in all steps in the appeal process, homeowners need to know the laws of their state and their rights with regard to property tax. And just like in the original appeal to the tax assessors, homeowners need to be certain that they protect their rights.

One of the ways to do that is to look at the "no change" notice from the tax assessors or the notice offering the reduction that was deemed unsatisfactory. Does the notice indicate what to do to further the appeal? In many cases, it does. If the notice doesn't provide instructions about how to appeal to the next level and give the deadline to make that appeal, then contact the tax assessor's office and ask them to explain the procedure. They should be willing to do this.

Board members are taxpayers like you
The second level of appeal is typically a board of equalization, board of review, board of appeals, appellate tax board, etc. (to keep this simple, let's refer to them as "Boards"). These Boards are usually made up of county or city taxpayers who have been schooled on the state's property tax law and are supposed to render an unbiased opinion of taxable value after hearing both sides of the argument. Some states have a state level board for a third level of appeal, and most states also allow appeals to the court system.

I recommend an appeal option that is free of cost, if there is a free option. In many states, Boards are free of charge to the taxpayer. Remember this though -- before you spend any money, there's always next year. In many states, you can appeal your property tax value every year. If you appeal next year there's a chance that a different county appraiser will be working your market area, or the same appraiser will have a sunnier disposition. Things may look different to the other side in 8 to 12 months, so you might want to save your money and try again later.

Board members often have to attend a multi-day course before they can sit on a board. Once they are on the Boards, they have to meet continuing education requirements. It may not be necessary to have a real estate background to sit on a Board, but some Board members do have such a background. The Boards also have administrative staff that organize the Boards, set dates for hearings, set times for hearings, deliver notices to taxpayers regarding the date and time of the hearings and send a notice of the decision regarding the taxable value.

Develop a presentation strategy

Typically, these Boards are composed of three-five members. Before appearing before one of these Boards, it is a good idea to know how many members are on a Board so the person making the appeal can give a copy of the presentation to each Board member. The Board will have a chairperson who does most of the talking and is often the dominant member of the board, although other members may speak. In general, the rules of a Board hearing are that each party gets to present their case uninterrupted by the other party. After the parties have finished making their cases, there is time for the Board members to ask questions. There is also time for the tax payer or the tax assessor personnel to rebut the various points that the other party made during their presentation.

I recommend that people making a presentation stay calm and confident during the hearing. I also think it's a good idea to speak to all members of the Board, although it may be best to concentrate on any dominant members because they tend to push the other members toward their way of thinking. Another good idea is to be firm and ask the Board to render the value that your data supports. Another strategy is to be accommodative if both sides have good information. For example, if you have good evidence supporting a value of $150,000 and the county has good evidence supporting a value of $200,000, you may want to tell the Board that a value of $175,000 would be acceptable to you. Willingness to compromise makes you look reasonable.

It's worth saying again that many states allow appeals to be made every year. So, even if the Board does not grant a satisfactory value, it may not be necessary to go to a third level of appeal. This is especially true if it's going to be costly to appeal further. Also, remember that a change in season or a change in county appraiser may result in a lower taxable value in the New Year.

Chapter 13
The court system

Most states allow homeowners to appeal their property tax assessment to the court system if they are not satisfied with the result from other appeal options. While those options are generally free, courts typically charge a filing fee to make a property tax appeal. The purpose of the fee is to keep frivolous lawsuits out of the courtroom. There is another hurdle to appealing through the court system. In my experience, judges do not want to deal with property tax appeals. Before they will hear a case, they will require the two parties to meet with a mediator to try and reach an agreement.

Before deciding to file a court appeal, it's important to ask yourself two questions.

1. Are you certain your tax assessment is too high?
2. Do you have strong evidence to support a lower value?

If the answers are yes, you should do a cost benefit analysis to see if a court appeal is in your best financial interests.

1. Subtract the current assessment from the desired assessment.
2. Apply the tax rate to the difference and calculate the tax savings you will receive if you are able to get the assessment reduction you are looking for.
3. Subtract your filing fee from the tax savings.
4. If the court system requires those making the appeal to be represented by an attorney, subtract the estimated attorney's fees from the estimated tax savings. If the court will allow you to argue the appeal yourself, you will have to ask yourself how you value your time. Subtract this cost from the potential tax savings.
5. Lastly, be sure to find out if the court wants an independent appraisal of the property. For a single family house, this might cost $300-$600. For a commercial property, it may cost thousands of dollars.

Many homeowners come to the conclusion that the cost of appealing to the court system overwhelms any potential tax savings. If it's "just the principle of the thing," don't let me stop you. However, for most taxpayers with limited funds, this may not be their best option. Again, I have to stress that most states allow homeowners to appeal their tax assessment every year. Give the process another chance before spending money you may not recoup.

Part 3: Grade A help

Chapter 14
Choosing a property tax consultant

What services does a property tax service provide? Firms such as mine:

1. Do a Sales Comparison Approach and/or a Cost Approach as well as, where appropriate, an Income Approach to put a value on your property.
2. Look at equity or uniformity to determine whether your property is assessed fairly compared to your neighbors or your competition.
3. Look at other benchmarks and statistics such as capitalization rates, units of comparison, operating expense ratios, etc.
4. Fill out all the paperwork.
5. File property tax returns if necessary
6. File the property tax appeals.
7. Meet all appropriate deadlines.
8. Prepare presentation materials for both the tax assessor and formal board hearings.
9. Do the "legwork" and inspect the property being appealed, and all comparables.
10. Meet with the assessment staff to discuss the appeal and try to get them to reduce the taxable value.
11. Attend formal hearings, if all else fails, to try and get the taxable value reduced.

Some property tax services also perform "compliance" work or personal property return work. Many states require property owners to "return" their personal property value for taxation, which is why it is referred to as "compliance." Some property tax services also perform tax bill processing. This is a service in which they check your tax bill for accuracy and then send it to you with an "okay to pay." And some analyze leases to make sure that the landlord is charging the tenant appropriately for common area maintenance fees and other charges.

Is a tax service right for me?

When do you need a property tax service? Ask yourself the following questions.

1. Do you have the time to do the research and determine whether your property tax assessment is reasonable?
2. Do you have the time needed to travel to and from the assessor's office or to and from a formal hearing?
3. Will you want to sink your money into the research tools needed to determine whether your property tax value is correct and find the information needed to get a lower value?
4. If you are an out-of-town owner, do you want to put money into traveling to and from the assessor's office and formal hearings?
5. Do you want to take time away from work?
6. Do you have appraisal knowledge? (This book counts!)
7. Do you know how mass appraisal differs from real estate appraisal and do you know what the mass appraisal standards are?
8. Do you have negotiation skills and are you comfortable negotiating?
9. Will you be comfortable giving a presentation at a formal hearing?
10. Will you be comfortable rebutting the presentation of the property tax assessor personnel?

All of these are things to think about when deciding whether to use a property tax appeal service.

How do I find a tax consultant?

When searching for a qualified property tax consultant, I recommend using the Internet and locally specific search key words. For example, if you live in Denver, search with these key words: "Denver property tax consultants." If you live in Portland, Maine, use this search: "Portland, Maine property tax consultants." If you don't refine your search with local parameters such as a city name, the search engines will bring up property tax services from all over the country. Once you have found a local firm, find out who will be handling your appeal and check their qualifications. Ask how long have they been in the business. Do they have a real estate background other than property tax appeal work? Ask for a resume or a qualifications brief.

During the recent real estate downturn, a lot of people got into property tax appeal work. Real estate agents used to be very busy five or six years ago. Suddenly, the real estate market turned from feast to famine. With less money coming in, some agents began offering property tax consulting services. There are real estate appraisers who don't have as much appraisal work as they used to, and some of them have become property tax consultants as well. Be aware that some people are not experienced long-time property tax consulting professionals and are only doing it on a part-time basis while they're waiting for their primary line of business to come back to life.

Property tax consultants with mass appraisal experience are often a good choice because they are very familiar with the tax assessor's processes for generating taxable values. Some very large companies like to use property tax consultants who are former assessors. Some property tax assessors choose property tax consulting as their next career.

Some people think that if they are going to appeal their property tax value that they need a real estate appraisal. This is probably a mistake. Appraisers have to render an unbiased opinion of value. That means they have to use the most comparable sales available to appraise your property, not the lowest sales available. Because they may not be using the lowest sale available, you may miss out on potential tax savings. If I'm working on a property tax appeal and I am not acting in the capacity of a real estate appraiser, I can use any data that I want. I can use the lowest sales available and be an advocate for my client, whereas the real estate appraiser cannot.

One way to find a property tax consultant that I have found to be effective is to ask the tax assessor's office to recommend someone. Tax assessors know the good property tax consultants from the bad ones. Tell the assessor that you don't have a lot of time for your appeal and that you don't understand real estate appraisals. Chances are good that they'll give you the name of a good consultant they like working with. It is highly unlikely that the tax assessor will give you the name of a property tax consultant who is unethical. Reputation is important. The tax assessment personnel know which consultants "cross the line."

Chapter 15
Results to be expected

Be wary of consultants who guarantee you tax savings. There is no such thing. If somebody tells you they will definitely be able to get your property tax reduced, run the other way. Contingent fees, in which the property tax consultant gets a percentage of any tax savings they generate, are the best way to go. Property tax consultants will often work high-valued properties for this type of arrangement. For residential appeals, they often charge an up-front fee as well.

Always look at a consultant's qualifications and consider someone local to work your property tax appeal. When we talk to national companies/property owners and they have property in, say, Wichita, Kansas, they will ask "who's your guy in Wichita?" They know that local property tax consultants have existing relationships with the property tax assessors in the area. So don't be hesitant to ask the property tax assessor's office to recommend a consultant they consider to be reputable.

Again, there is no guarantee in this business, because it is all about people working with people, negotiating to come up with a value estimate that makes sense based on the market and the local tax law. People have different personalities and different experiences. You never know what you're going to get. One day you can walk into the tax assessor's office to work with Joe, and he can be very accommodative. It may be easy to work out a reduction with him. The next week Joe's having a bad day. He likes his sale ratio statistics in the neighborhood. He thinks the values are fair and refuses to change the value.

In conclusion, get local expertise, check resumes and look at qualifications. There is no guarantee that you can get a property tax assessment reduction, but you can improve your chances by carefully selecting the person or company that is going to make the appeal on your behalf.

Chapter 16
Information to be provided

If your house was appraised in the last few years, please provide information about that appraisal to your tax consultant. Even if the information is too old to use in your current property tax appeal, the appraisal could contain information that will help support your case for a tax reduction. If you listed your property for sale and then took it off the market for whatever reason -- maybe it didn't sell or you didn't get a decent offer -- give the consultant that information as well. Did you have your house inspected when you purchased it? If the inspection report isn't a very old document, share that. Any interior photos that you'd like to have considered, especially photos of detrimental conditions such as water damage, termite damage, or deferred maintenance of any kind, may also help the consultant.

Appraisals should also be provided to consultants working on commercial property tax appeals. To complete Income Approaches to value, the consultant will need income and expense statements from the prior year. Most states have an effective date of appraisal for property tax purposes of January 1. So, if a consultant is working on a 2013 property tax appeal, he or she will need the income and expense data from year 2012 and a rent roll from as close to January 1 of 2013 as possible. Just as with residential appeals, if the commercial property was listed for sale and it didn't sell, please provide the consultant with information related to the listing. Current listings for sale or rent, or written offers for sale or rent, are also important.

Always be accommodative. Your tax consultant is on your side. The data associated with your property is very important when trying to get a property tax reduction. The tax assessor is estimating market value, so they want to use market data or data from the market as a whole, but they will consider data from individual properties, and that can make a big difference.

Chapter 17
Cost/benefit of a property tax service

The cost for residential property tax appeal consulting falls in a narrow range. A typical residential flat fee may be $350 or higher. Alternatively, many companies charge $250 up front and 25 percent of the tax savings generated. Some charge $150 plus a third of the tax savings generated. Generally speaking, I consider the consultant's qualifications to be more important than saving a few dollars in up-front costs. Your best bet is to find the most qualified consultant that you can.

Beware of companies that send you a letter or postcard with a calculation proclaiming "this is how much we think we can save you." You can be reasonably certain that they are using a database of old values to generate these postcard savings estimates, especially if you get it right after you get your assessment notice. I would be very cautious about responding to such an unsolicited mailing, especially if there's a high flat fee involved. Some of these charges may be $350 or more. If you're in a city or county that reappraises on an annual basis, spending that much money may be a losing proposition. If the company gets a reduction that doesn't cover their service fees and the county increases your tax assessment the next year, then you have just wasted your money.

Commercial properties
Commercial property tax appeal costs also fall in a narrow range. So, again, I would look at qualifications. The dollars that you might save probably aren't worth going with the low-cost provider. If you have a high-value commercial property, you can probably get a property tax appeal done on a contingent basis (percentage of the tax savings). Some consultants charge an upfront fee of $250 and 25 percent of tax savings for lower value properties. Many consultants will do tax appeal work on high-value properties for strictly 25-33 percent of the tax savings.

Why not choose a firm that will give you a free consultation? A good firm will take a look at your value and give you an idea of whether there are potential tax savings in filing an appeal. Then you can do a cost-benefit analysis to decide whether it's worth it to engage the firm.

Factor in your own time

You can also do a cost-benefit analysis that includes your own time. Then you can decide whether you want to appeal the tax assessment yourself or whether you want to pay someone to do it. Take a look at how much tax savings you might be able to generate, and how much time it might take you to prepare a property tax appeals case and drive to the tax assessor's office to talk to the county appraiser. And if that appeal fails, think about how much additional time/expense you will incur by driving to a formal board hearing to argue your case. Based on how you value your own time, and any time away from work, subtract your cost from the potential tax savings. You may have to take into account the number of years the reduction might hold. Now you can look at your cost, the cost of the consultant and, based on the potential tax savings, make an informed decision.

Property tax consultants will do everything they can to get your property tax burden reduced. They will use multiple approaches to value to see if they can find one that supports a lower value. They will look at equity to see if the property tax assessment is unfair and whether they can get it reduced that way. There are no guarantees, however.

Some real estate owners don't want to pay an up-front fee for a property tax service. The reasons property tax consultants charge an up-front fee include research tools, time and travel expense. Also, residential values are generally too low to do this work on a straight contingent fee basis. Paying a property tax consultant is similar to paying a real estate appraiser up front. The appraiser wants to be paid first because he (she) knows that if you don't like their value estimate you are less likely to pay.

Part 4: Conclusion and appendix

Chapter 18
Final words

I hope you found this book informative and somewhat inspiring. Although the property tax appeal process can seem daunting, it doesn't need to be. Just do the research to determine whether your tax assessment is too high, and you're on your way. Some people wonder if appealing their tax assessment will result in retaliatory steps by the assessor. This is very unlikely. The appeal process is there for a reason, the mass appraisal process is inaccurate. Any assessor who holds an appeal against you doesn't know, or deserve, their job.

I will continue to help taxpayers help themselves. For updates, please check our Fair Assessments website often and read our Fair Assessments Now! blog regularly. I will continue to post worthwhile resources I find that support property tax appeals. You can also help others by by posting tax appeal tactics on the blog that you have used successfully. In addition, I'll also post other information I create, like this book, on the website so that it will continue to be a tax appeals resource for residential and commercial property owners.

All the best,

Daniel Thomas Jones

Appendix – State Resources

Alabama

http://revenue.alabama.gov/advalorem/

Alaska

http://www.commerce.state.ak.us/dca/logon/tax/tax-prop.htm

Arizona

http://www.azdor.gov/PropertyTax.aspx

Arkansas

http://www.arkansas.gov/acd/index.html

California

http://www.boe.ca.gov/lawguides/property/current/ptlg/property-taxes-law-guide.html

Colorado

http://www.colorado.gov/cs/Satellite/DOLA-Main/CBON/1251590375296

Connecticut

http://www.jud.ct.gov/lawlib/law/taxappeal.htm

Delaware

By County:

http://www3.nccde.org/parcel/search/
http://www.co.kent.de.us/Departments/Finance/assessment.htm
http://www.sussexcountyde.gov/dept/assessment/

District of Columbia

http://otr.cfo.dc.gov/otr/cwp/view,a,1330,q,594366.asp

Florida

http://www.stateofflorida.com/Portal/DesktopDefault.aspx?tabid=29

Georgia

https://etax.dor.ga.gov/ptd/adm/law/index.aspx

Hawaii

http://www6.hawaii.gov/tax/a4_2hrs.htm

Idaho

http://tax.idaho.gov/p-propertytax.cfm

Illinois

http://tax.illinois.gov/LocalGovernment/PropertyTax/

Indiana

http://www.in.gov/dlgf/2516.htm

Iowa

http://www.iowa.gov/tax/educate/78573.html

Kansas

http://www.ksrevenue.org/pvd.html

Kentucky

http://revenue.ky.gov/Property+Tax/

Louisiana

http://www.latax.state.la.us/

Maine

http://www.maine.gov/revenue/propertytax/propertytaxlaw/propertytaxlaw.htm

Maryland

http://dat.state.md.us/

Massachusetts

http://www.lawlib.state.ma.us/subject/about/propertytax.html

Michigan

http://www.michigan.gov/taxes/0,1607,7-238-43535---,00.html

Minnesota

http://www.revenue.state.mn.us/propertytax/Pages/Tax-Information.aspx

Mississippi

http://www.dor.ms.gov/taxareas/property/main.html

Missouri

http://www.stc.mo.gov/

Montana

http://revenue.mt.gov/forindividuals/property-owners.mcpx

Nebraska

http://www.revenue.ne.gov/PAD/

Nevada

http://tax.state.nv.us/DOAS_MAIN.htm

New Hampshire

http://www.nh.gov/btla/appeals/propertytax.htm

New Jersey

http://www.state.nj.us/treasury/taxation/lpt/localtax.shtml

New Mexico

http://www.tax.newmexico.gov/about-us/property-tax-division/Pages/Home.aspx

New York

http://www.tax.ny.gov/pit/property/

North Carolina

http://www.dor.state.nc.us/taxes/property/index.html

North Dakota

http://www.nd.gov/tax/property/

Ohio

http://www.caao.org/DIRECTORY/

Oklahoma

http://www.tax.ok.gov/

Oregon

http://www.oregon.gov/DOR/PTD/Pages/property.aspx

Pennsylvania

http://www.lgc.state.pa.us/ccal.shtml

Rhode Island

http://www.dor.ri.gov/muniinfo/

South Carolina

http://www.sctax.org/Tax+Information/property/default.htm

South Dakota

http://www.state.sd.us/drr2/propspectax/property/home.htm

Tennessee

http://www.comptroller.tn.gov/pa/index.asp

Texas

http://www.window.state.tx.us/taxinfo/proptax/

Utah

http://propertytax.utah.gov/real-property.html

Vermont

http://www.sec.state.vt.us/municipal/handbooks.htm

Virginia

http://leg1.state.va.us/cgi-bin/legp504.exe?000+cod+TOC58010000032000000000000

Washington

http://dor.wa.gov/content/findtaxesandrates/propertytax/prop_rnls.aspx

West Virginia

http://www.state.wv.us/taxrev/ptdweb/tax-codes.htm

Wisconsin

http://www.revenue.wi.gov/faqs/index-pt.html

Wyoming

http://revenue.wyo.gov/property-tax-division

About the Author

Daniel Jones is a property tax consultant, entrepreneur, real estate appraiser, and investor. He is the managing director and founder of Fair Assessments, LLC. His company saves real estate owners, managers, and tenants hundreds of thousands annually. Dan has been in real estate valuation services for over 20 years as a fee appraiser, a tax assessor for counties in Virginia and Georgia, and as a property tax reduction professional for the last nine years. He holds the RES designation awarded by the International Association of Assessing Officers. Dan's inside knowledge of how the tax assessors generate their taxable values gives him the edge in value negotiations.

Made in the USA
Lexington, KY
28 May 2016